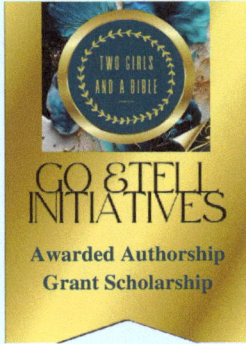

It is a true honor to award Lucas Sanchez with our Authors scholarship, recognizing his commitment and the commitment of his family to becoming an author who glorifies our Lord and Savior, Jesus Christ.

Our mission is to "Go and Tell" the incredible stories that Jesus is writing on hearts today. Lucas Sanchez exemplifies a heart dedicated to serving the Kingdom of God through the unique gifts and talents the Lord has given him. We are profoundly thankful to witness the magnificent work the Lord is accomplishing in and through the dedicated efforts of Lucas Sanchez and his family.

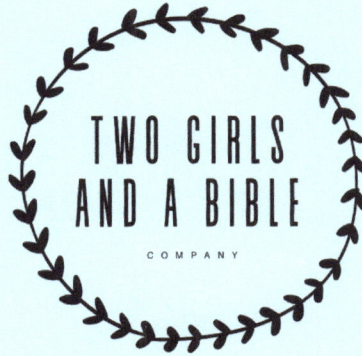

We are a 501c3 Nonprofit organization called to "Go and Tell." Our children's books are based on real life testimonies of children, parents, and grandparents, family members and friends. All proceeds help us propagate the Gospel of Jesus Christ to reach the world with the Gospel of Faith, Hope, and Love, but most importantly Love!

30 Days in the Bible with lil Luke

2025 Authors, Luke Sanchez and Pancho Sanchez, Contributions by Michael McPherson, Illustrated by Olivia Kim and Ani Inoyo, Consultant and Production, by Jennifer C Tabora and Kimberly Receveur with Two Girls and a Bible, Division Publishing.

Published By Two Girls and a Bible, Inc. A registered Trademark.

Publishing Award presented to Luke Sanchez and Pancho Sanchez through the Authorship Scholarship Program of the "Go and Tell" Initiatives of Two Girls and a Bible, Inc., Fulfilling the call to share the stories Jesus is writing on hearts today!

Published in Cape Coral, Florida, by Two Girls and a Bible, Inc., which is a registered trademark.

Two Girls and a Bible titles may be purchased in bulk for educational, business, fund-raising, or sales promotional use. For more information, please email SpecialMarkets@twogirlsandabible.org.

ISBN: 979-8-9929798-1-7
Print, paperback, family, biblical commentaries, transferable as children's literature, non-fiction

Library of Congress Cataloging in Publication Data is on File.

Printed by KDP. Reproduced in Canva, illustrations by Olivia Kim and Ani Inoyo, gtmagazine@twogirlsandabible.org, authorized use through subscription certificates.
Books › Children's Books › Religions › Inspirational

FOREWORD

HEY THERE, YOUNG READER!

GET READY FOR AN ADVENTURE FULL OF WONDER AND WISDOM! AS YOU FLIP THROUGH THE PAGES OF THIS DEVOTIONAL BOOK, YOU'RE DIVING INTO THE BIBLE, ONE OF THE COOLEST STORIES EVER TOLD.

THE BIBLE ISN'T JUST A BUNCH OF OLD WRITINGS; IT'S A LIVING STORY ABOUT GOD'S LOVE, GRACE, AND POWER. THIS BOOK IS MADE JUST FOR YOU, TO HELP YOU UNDERSTAND THE BIBLE'S TIMELESS LESSONS. EACH DAY, YOU'LL READ A BIT FROM THE BIBLE AND THEN THINK ABOUT HOW IT FITS INTO YOUR LIFE. THESE REFLECTIONS WILL MAKE YOU THINK DEEPLY, ASK QUESTIONS, AND GROW IN YOUR FAITH.

REMEMBER, THE BIBLE IS NOT JUST A BOOK TO READ—IT'S A GUIDE TO LIVE BY. THE STORIES AND TEACHINGS INSIDE ARE HERE TO INSPIRE YOU TO BE KIND, SEEK JUSTICE, AND STAY HUMBLE. WHETHER YOU'RE FACING SCHOOL CHALLENGES, FRIENDSHIPS, OR JUST FIGURING OUT THE WORLD, THE BIBLE OFFERS HELP AND COMFORT.

THIS DEVOTIONAL JOURNEY IS ALSO A CHANCE TO CONNECT WITH YOUR FAMILY AND CHURCH. SHARE THE STORIES YOU READ WITH THOSE AROUND YOU. TALKING ABOUT THESE TRUTHS WITH PARENTS, SIBLINGS, AND FRIENDS CAN MAKE YOUR FAITH EVEN STRONGER.

REMEMBER, EVERY TIME YOU OPEN THIS BOOK, YOU'RE NOT ALONE. YOU'RE JOINING COUNTLESS OTHERS WHO HAVE TURNED TO THE BIBLE FOR GUIDANCE AND COMFORT THROUGHOUT THE AGES.

SO, TAKE A DEEP BREATH, OPEN YOUR HEART, AND DIVE INTO THE STORIES THAT HAVE SHAPED THE FAITH OF MILLIONS. LET EACH PAGE GUIDE YOU ON YOUR SPIRITUAL JOURNEY, HELPING YOU UNDERSTAND GOD'S LOVE FOR YOU AND THE WHOLE WORLD.

PASTOR BRIAN ATKINS, LIFE CHURCH

ENDORSEMENT

I AM SO EXCITED TO SHARE THIS BOOK WITH MY KIDS AND MY CHURCH! IT'S A FANTASTIC BLEND OF FAITH AND FUN STORYTELLING THAT HELPS KIDS GROW SPIRITUALLY.

EACH DAILY REFLECTION IS EASY TO UNDERSTAND AND BEAUTIFULLY ILLUSTRATED, DRAWING KIDS INTO THE STORIES AND TEACHINGS. THE LANGUAGE IS CLEAR, MAKING SPIRITUAL IDEAS SIMPLE FOR YOUNG READERS.

PARENTS AND TEACHERS WILL FIND THIS BOOK SUPER HELPFUL. IT SPARKS MEANINGFUL CONVERSATIONS AND IS PERFECT FOR FAMILY READING TIME.

IN A WORLD FULL OF DISTRACTIONS, THIS DEVOTIONAL IS A GUIDE FOR YOUNG HEARTS. I TRULY BELIEVE IT WILL MAKE A BIG IMPACT AND HELP KIDS DEVELOP A LASTING LOVE FOR JESUS!

PASTOR BRIAN ATKINS, LIFE CHURCH

DID YOU KNOW THAT GOD DOESN'T LOOK DOWN ON YOU BECAUSE YOU'RE YOUNG?

THE BIBLE TEACHES US THAT WE CAN BE A GOOD EXAMPLE FOR THE PEOPLE AROUND US BY HOW WE SPEAK AND ACT TO EACH OTHER!

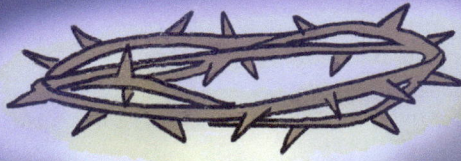

DO YOU KNOW HOW MUCH
GOD LOVES YOU?

HE LOVES YOU SO MUCH THAT HE
SENT HIS SON JESUS CHRIST TO DIE
FOR YOUR SINS AND MINE!

ALL WE HAVE TO DO IS
CONFESS AND BELIEVE IN HIM AND
WE WILL HAVE ETERNAL LIFE.

**THIS IS THE GREATEST ACT
OF LOVE EVER DONE!**

FOR GOD SO LOVED THE WORLD, THAT HE GAVE HIS ONLY SON,

THAT WHOEVER BELIEVES IN HIM WILL NOT PERISH, BUT HAVE ETERNAL LIFE. JOHN 3:16

DAY 3

FOR WE ARE GOD'S HANDIWORK, CREATED IN CHRIST JESUS TO DO GOOD WORKS, WHICH GOD PREPARED IN ADVANCE FOR US TO DO.

EPHESIANS 2:10

"WE ARE GOD'S HANDIWORK"

WE ARE CREATED BY GOD, JUST LIKE AN ARTIST PAINTS BEAUTIFUL PAINTINGS, GOD CREATED US IN A BEAUTIFUL WAY.

HE MADE US EXACTLY THE WAY HE INTENDED, ON PURPOSE!

SOMETIMES, WE MAY NOT LIKE CERTAIN THINGS ABOUT OURSELVES, BUT HE CREATED US THIS WAY FOR A REASON — A PURPOSE WE WILL UNDERSTAND ONE DAY.

SOMETIMES WE GO THROUGH
MOMENTS WHEN EVERYTHING SEEMS
DARK AND SCARY, BUT GOD WANTS TO
REMIND US THAT EVEN IN THOSE
DARKEST TIMES, HE IS WITH US.

NOT ONLY IS HE THERE
WITH US, BUT HE ALSO GIVES US
WHAT WE NEED TO FEEL COMFORTED
DURING THOSE TIMES.

PRAY TO GOD, ASK HIM FOR
PEACE, AND HE WILL COMFORT YOU.

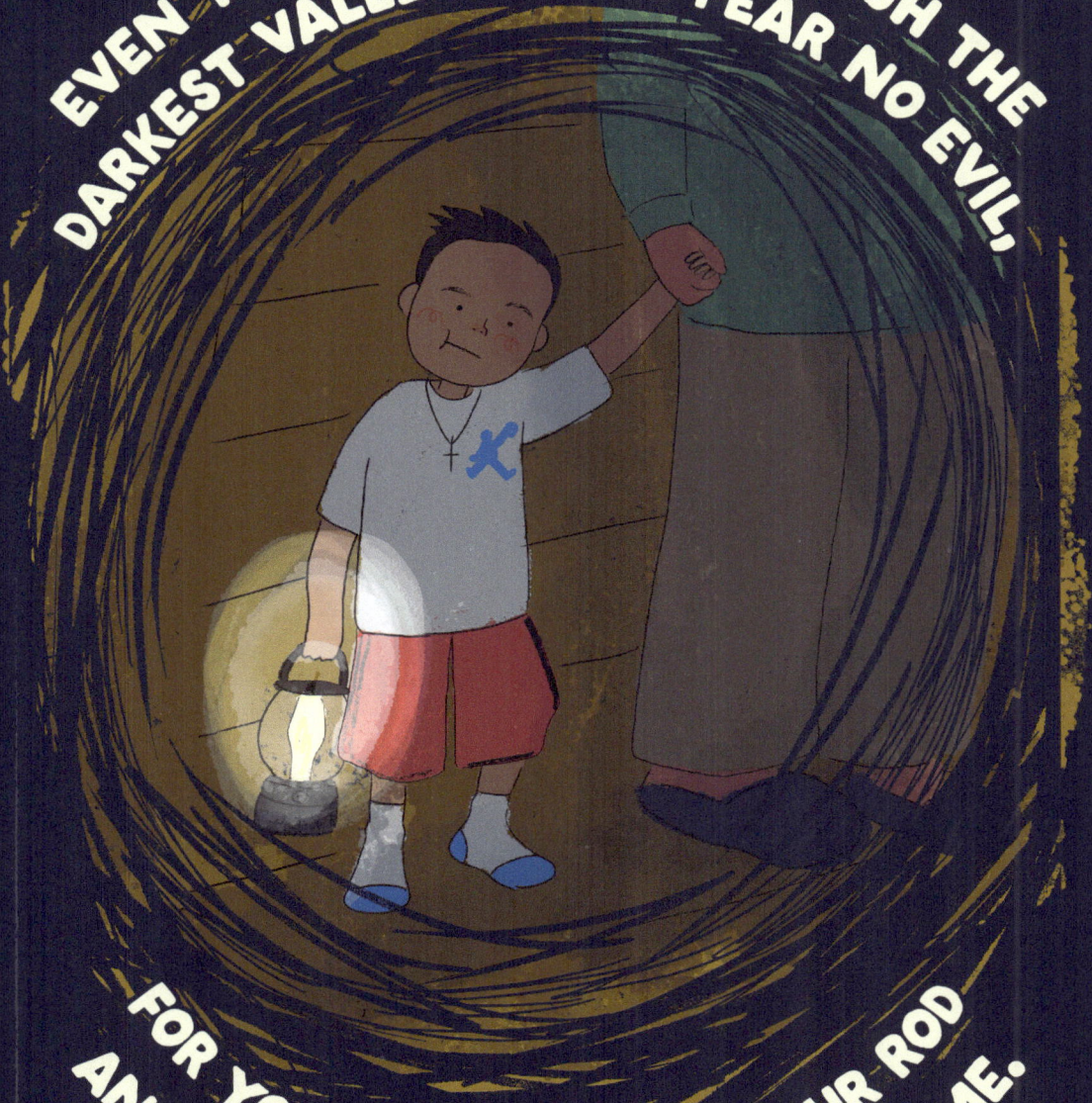

EVEN THOUGH I WALK THROUGH THE DARKEST VALLEY I WILL FEAR NO EVIL, FOR YOU ARE WITH ME, YOUR ROD AND YOUR STAFF, THEY COMFORT ME. PSALM 23:4

GOD'S PLANS FOR US ARE ALWAYS GOOD IN THE END.

EVEN WHEN THINGS ARE NOT GOING THE
WAY WE WANT THEM TO, THEY ARE GOING
THE WAY GOD WANTS THEM TO.

BUT GOD REMINDED THEM
THAT THERE IS A BRIGHT FUTURE AND
HOPE AHEAD WHEN WE TRUST IN HIM.

PAUL SHARED THIS SCRIPTURE BECAUSE IT WAS IMPORTANT TO REMIND PEOPLE THAT JESUS IS THE SON OF GOD AND THE WAY TO SALVATION.

THERE WILL BE TIMES IN OUR LIVES WHEN WE MIGHT FEEL EMBARRASSED ABOUT GOING TO CHURCH OR BELIEVING IN GOD, BUT THIS VERSE REMINDS US NOT TO BE ASHAMED.

FOR I AM NOT ASHAMED OF THE GOSPEL, BECAUSE IT IS THE POWER OF GOD THAT BRINGS SALVATION TO EVERYONE WHO BELIEVES

ROMANS 1:16

DO NOT BE OVERCOME
BY EVIL, BUT OVERCOME
EVIL WITH GOOD.

ROMANS 12:21

EVEN WHEN BAD THINGS HAPPEN AROUND US, THE BIBLE REMINDS US THAT THERE'S ALWAYS AN OPPORTUNITY TO HONOR GOD!

CAN YOU BELIEVE THAT JESUS
SAID ADULTS NEED TO BECOME LIKE
CHILDREN TO ENTER HEAVEN?

HE SAID THIS BECAUSE CHILDREN
ARE INNOCENT, CURIOUS, HUMBLE,
AND NOT FOCUSED ON CHASING
THINGS LIKE MONEY OR FAME.

SOMETIMES, ADULTS CAN
GET A LITTLE DISTRACTED!

HE CALLED A LITTLE CHILD TO HIM,
AND PLACED THE CHILD AMONG THEM.
AND HE SAID:

"TRULY I TELL YOU, UNLESS YOU
CHANGE AND BECOME LIKE LITTLE
CHILDREN, YOU WILL NEVER ENTER
THE KINGDOM OF HEAVEN."

MATTHEW 18:2-4

DAY 9

IF GOD IS FOR US, WHO CAN BE AGAINST US?

ROMANS 8:31

IF THE CREATOR OF THE UNIVERSE IS YOUR FRIEND, SUPPORTER, AND HEAVENLY FATHER, WHO CAN STAND AGAINST YOU?

THIS DOES NOT MEAN YOU CAN DO WHATEVER YOU WANT, WHENEVER YOU WANT, BUT IT DOES MEAN THAT WHEN YOUR PLANS ALIGN WITH HIS, NOTHING CAN STOP THEM.

WHEN GOD GAVE THE TEN COMMANDMENTS AT THE BEGINNING OF THE BIBLE, MANY OF THEM WERE SIMPLE INSTRUCTIONS.

THE FIRST ONE WITH A PROMISE WAS: "HONOR YOUR FATHER AND MOTHER."

GOD SAID THAT IF YOU DO THIS, YOUR DAYS WILL BE LONG ON THE EARTH.

THIS SHOWS HOW IMPORTANT IT IS TO HONOR, RESPECT, AND OBEY OUR PARENTS!

"HONOR YOUR FATHER AND MOTHER"
(THIS IS THE FIRST COMMANDMENT WITH A PROMISE)

"THAT IT MAY GO WELL WITH YOU AND THAT YOU MAY LIVE LONG IN THE LAND."

EPHESIANS 6:2-3

SOME PEOPLE SAY THAT THEY KNOW GOD
BUT THEY DO NOT LOVE PEOPLE WELL.

A GOOD WAY TO KNOW IF SOMEONE IS
CLOSE TO GOD IS TO SEE HOW KIND AND
LOVING THEY ARE TO OTHER PEOPLE.

JESUS WAS SO LOVING THAT HE ACTUALLY
CONFUSED THE DISCIPLES WITH HIS KINDNESS
TOWARDS BOTH BELIEVERS AND SINNERS.

EPHESIANS 4:32

BE KIND TO ONE ANOTHER, TENDERHEARTED, FORGIVING ONE ANOTHER, AS GOD IN CHRIST FORGAVE YOU.

WOULDN'T IT BE AMAZING IF EVERYONE WAS NICE TO EACH OTHER?

WHAT IF EVERYONE AT SCHOOL, CHURCH AND HOME TRIED THEIR BEST TO BE KIND?

THAT WOULD BE AN AMAZING WORLD!

HOW CAN A YOUNG PERSON STAY ON THE PATH OF PURITY? BY LIVING ACCORDING TO YOUR WORD.

PSALM 119:9

WHAT'S THE SECRET TO LIVING A GREAT LIFE? READ THE BIBLE AND LIVE ACCORDING TO ITS TEACHINGS.

WE ALL THINK WE KNOW
THE BEST WAY TO DO THINGS.

BUT THIS PROVERB OR WISE
SAYING LETS US KNOW WE SHOULD
REALLY PUT OUR TRUST IN THE
LORD AND NOT OUR OWN BRAINS.

THE NEXT TIME YOU HAVE
TO MAKE A DECISION ASK THE
LORD WHAT <u>HE</u> THINKS YOU
SHOULD DO FIRST.

IT MAY NOT FEEL LIKE IT,
BUT THERE IS <u>ALWAYS</u>
A REASON TO THANK GOD.

THROUGH THE
GOOD TIMES AND HARD TIMES,
ALWAYS REJOICE!

WHEN YOU ARE NERVOUS
OR AFRAID, REMEMBER YOU CAN
PUT YOUR TRUST IN GOD.

NO PROBLEM IS

TOO BIG

OR TOO SMALL

FOR GOD

BECAUSE HE LOVES US SO MUCH!

DAY 17

ELEMENTARY SCHOOL

HOME 56 1.0

AWAY 56 4TH

I CAN DO ALL THINGS THROUGH HIM WHO STRENGTHENS ME.

PHILIPPIANS 4:13

THERE IS NO LIMIT
TO WHAT WE CAN DO
THROUGH JESUS!

THAT DOESN'T
MEAN WE CAN FLY
LIKE SUPERHEROES BUT
WHATEVER GOD WANTS TO DO
WITH YOU HE WILL MAKE SURE
YOU CAN GET IT DONE!

1ST PLACE

DAY 18

EVERYONE WILL DEAL
    WITH STRESS AND ANXIETY
    AT SOME POINT IN THEIR LIVES.

WHEN WE ARE REALLY
    STRESSED OUT
    MOST TIMES IT IS SOMETHING
    THAT IS BEYOND OUR CONTROL.

WHEN WE LEARN TO
    GIVE GOD OUR PROBLEMS
    NOT ONLY DO WE LET GO OF
    OUR STRESS BUT WE LET GOD
    KNOW WE TRUST HIM TO TAKE
    CONTROL OF OUR LIVES.

"Ah am fealfuwy and wondufly made!"
(translation: I am fearfully and wonderfully made!)

I PRAISE YOU BECAUSE I AM FEARFULLY AND WONDERFULLY MADE; YOUR WORKS ARE WONDERFUL, I KNOW THAT FULL WELL.

PSALM 139:14

GOD LOVED US FIRST!

THE BEST REASON TO LOVE HIM
IS BECAUSE HE LOVED US
EVEN BEFORE WE KNEW HIM!

DAY 21

DO TO OTHERS AS YOU WOULD HAVE THEM DO TO YOU.

LUKE 6:31

IMAGINE IF EVERYONE IN THE
WORLD TREATED EACH OTHER
WITH KINDNESS

THERE WOULD BE
NO STEALING
OR FIGHTING
OR BULLYING
OR LYING
.
.
BECAUSE
EVERYONE
WOULD BE NICE
TO EACH OTHER.

THE WHOLE WORLD
MAY NOT TREAT PEOPLE NICE,
BUT YOU AND I CAN!

DAY 22

WHEN WE READ THE BIBLE THE WORD GETS SAVED IN OUR HEARTS.

THE MORE WE READ IT THE MORE WE GET TO KNOW GOD AND HOW HE WANTS US TO LIVE!

I HAVE HIDDEN YOUR WORD IN MY HEART THAT I MIGHT NOT SIN AGAINST YOU.

PSALM 119:11

UNFORTUNATELY, EVERYONE
WILL HAVE A TIME IN THEIR LIFE
WHERE THEY SIN OR DISAPPOINT
GOD WITH THEIR ACTIONS.

THE GOOD NEWS IS THAT HE
KNOWS THAT AND HE STILL
LOVES US!

PAUL IS LETTING US KNOW
GOD WILL FORGIVE US WHEN
WE TURN AWAY FROM SIN
AND TURN TOWARD HIM.

IF GOD'S LOVE ENDURES
FOREVER THAT MEANS HE
WILL NEVER STOP LOVING
YOU AND ME.

EVEN WHEN WE MAKE
MISTAKES HE STILL LOVES US.
WE SHOULD LOVE HIM BACK
AND HONOR HIM WITH
OUR CHOICES.

IN THE BIBLE, WHEN THEY CHOSE KINGS, THEY ALWAYS EXPECTED THEM TO BE TALL, STRONG AND HANDSOME.

WHEN GOD CHOSE DAVID TO BE KING, EVERYONE WAS CONFUSED BECAUSE HE WAS THE SMALLEST AND LEAST IMPRESSIVE OF HIS WHOLE FAMILY BUT GOD CHOSE HIM ANYWAY.

GOD TEACHES US THAT WHAT IMPRESSES HIM IS ON THE INSIDE NOT THE OUTSIDE.

IT'S MORE BLESSED TO GIVE THAN TO RECEIVE.

ACTS 20:35

THINK ABOUT HOW MUCH YOU LOVE TO GET A GOOD GIFT.

THE BIBLE TELLS US THAT BEING ABLE TO GIVE A GIFT IS BETTER THAN TO RECEIVE A GIFT.

IT'S A BLESSING WHICH MEANS THAT IT'S SOMETHING THAT MAKES GOD HAPPY WHEN WE DO IT.

IT'S A GIFT TO GIVE!

NOTHING IS HARDER IN THIS LIFE THAN HAVING TO FORGIVE SOMEONE WHO HAS DONE SOMETHING WRONG TO YOU.

THE ONLY THING THAT MIGHT BE HARDER IS WHEN YOU DID SOMETHING WRONG TO SOMEONE AND YOU'RE HOPING THAT THEY WILL FORGIVE YOU.

JESUS SHOWS US HOW TO BE TRULY FORGIVING WHEN HE ASKED GOD TO FORGIVE THE PEOPLE THAT HURT HIM.

DAY 29

CHORES, HOMEWORK, SPORTS...

THE BIBLE TELLS US TO ALWAYS DO OUR BEST!

FOCUS

WE DO EVERYTHING LIKE WE'RE DOING IT FOR GOD, NOT JUST THE PEOPLE WE SEE.

WHATEVER YOU DO, WORK AT IT WITH ALL YOUR HEART, AS WORKING FOR THE LORD, NOT FOR HUMANS

COLOSSIANS 3:23

DAY 30

FOR WITH GOD,
NOTHING
WILL BE IMPOSSIBLE.

LUKE 1:37

THROUGHOUT THE BIBLE GOD
CAUSES MANY AMAZING THINGS
CALLED MIRACLES TO HAPPEN.

IN THIS SCRIPTURE AN ANGEL
TELLS MARY THAT SHE WILL
BE JESUS' MOTHER BUT NOT
ONLY THAT, HER COUSIN
WHO WAS NEVER ABLE
TO HAVE A BABY WAS
ALSO GOING TO BE
A MOTHER.

BOTH OF THE MOTHERS
THOUGHT THAT THIS WAS
IMPOSSIBLE BUT THE ANGEL
LETS HER KNOW WITH GOD
NOTHING IS IMPOSSIBLE.

ABOUT THE ILLUSTRATORS

THIS TALENTED DUO BRINGS THE PAGES OF THIS CHILDREN'S DEVOTIONAL TO LIFE WITH HEART AND IMAGINATION.

OLIVIA KIM'S WHIMSICAL AND EXPRESSIVE ILLUSTRATIONS CAPTURE THE WONDER AND JOY OF CHILDHOOD, WHILE ANI INOYO'S PLAYFUL YET POLISHED GRAPHIC DESIGN WEAVES EACH IMAGE SEAMLESSLY INTO THE BOOK'S THOUGHTFUL LAYOUT.

TOGETHER, THEY CREATE A VIBRANT VISUAL EXPERIENCE THAT INVITES YOUNG READERS TO EXPLORE FAITH WITH CURIOSITY AND DELIGHT.

FOLLOW THEIR WORK ON INSTAGRAM:
   @OLIVDAILY (OLIVIA KIM)
   @ANIDESIGNHOUSE (ANI INOYO)

ABOUT THE AUTHOR

LUCAS SANCHEZ, KNOWN AS LIL LUKE, WAS BORN IN 2016 IN THE SUNSHINE STATE OF FLORIDA. FROM THE VERY BEGINNING, HIS FAMILY SENSED THAT GOD HAD A SPECIAL PURPOSE FOR HIS LIFE.

AS A BABY, LUKE FACED A SERIOUS HEALTH CHALLENGE WHEN HE WAS HOSPITALIZED WITH RSV (RESPIRATORY SYNCYTIAL VIRUS) AND SPENT TWO WEEKS IN THE ICU. IT WAS A SCARY TIME—BUT ONE NIGHT, SOMETHING MIRACULOUS HAPPENED. LUKE MADE A FULL RECOVERY, AND HIS PARENTS KNEW THAT GOD WASN'T FINISHED WITH HIS STORY.

GROWING UP, LUKE HAS ALWAYS LOVED THE OUTDOORS, AND LIKE MANY KIDS, HE HAD A BIG COLLECTION OF HOT WHEELS. BUT AT JUST THREE YEARS OLD, SOMETHING SPECIAL CAUGHT HIS HEART—CHRISTIAN RAP MUSIC. FROM THAT MOMENT ON, HE DEVELOPED A PASSION NOT ONLY FOR MUSIC, BUT ALSO FOR SHARING HIS TESTIMONY AND PERFORMING FOR OTHERS.

NOW 8 YEARS OLD, LIL LUKE CONTINUES TO CHASE HIS CALLING. WHETHER HE'S ON STAGE RAPPING ABOUT HIS FAITH OR OUT FISHING AND SHOOTING HOOPS, ONE THING STAYS THE SAME—LUKE LOVES JESUS, AND HE LOVES OTHERS. HE LIVES OUT THE GREATEST COMMANDMENT: TO LOVE GOD AND LOVE PEOPLE.

www.ingramcontent.com/pod-product-compliance
Lightning Source LLC
Chambersburg PA
CBHW042010080426
42734CB00002B/33